VOTING

Published in the United States of America by Cherry Lake Publishing
Ann Arbor, Michigan
www.cherrylakepublishing.com

Content Adviser: Austin McCoy, Doctoral Candidate in History at the University of Michigan
Reading Adviser: Marla Conn MS, Ed., Literacy specialist, Read-Ability, Inc.

Photo Credits: © Marilyn Nieves/istock, cover, 1; © Joseph Sohm/Shutterstock, 5, 6, 24, 26; © Joshua Rainey Photography/
Shutterstock, 8; © Everett Historical/Shutterstock, 10, 20; © John Gomez/Shutterstock, 12; © My Lil' Rotten/Flickr, 15;
© Library of Congress, 16; © Louis Dalrymple/Library of Congress, 18; © Edmonston, Washington, D.C. (Photographer)/
Library of Congress, 19; © Rawpixel.com/Shutterstock, 23; © Lisa F. Young/Shutterstock, 28

Library of Congress Cataloging-in-Publication Data
Names: Mara, Wil, author.
Title: Voting / Wil Mara.
Description: Ann Arbor, Michigan : Cherry Lake Publishing, 2017. | Series: A citizen's guide |
    Audience: Grade 4 to 6. | Includes bibliographical references and index.
Identifiers: LCCN 2016001518| ISBN 9781634710725 (hardcover) | ISBN 9781634711715 (pdf) |
    ISBN 9781634712705 (pbk.) | ISBN 9781634713696 (ebook)
Subjects: LCSH: Voting—United States—Juvenile literature. | Elections—United States—Juvenile literature.
Classification: LCC JK1978 .M364 2017 | DDC 324.60973—dc23
LC record available at http://lccn.loc.gov/2016001518

Cherry Lake Publishing would like to acknowledge the work of the Partnership for 21st Century Learning.
Please visit *www.p21.org* for more information.

Printed in the United States of America
Corporate Graphics

ABOUT THE AUTHOR

Wil Mara is an award-winning and best-selling author of more than 150 books, many of which are educational titles for young readers. Further information about his work can be found at www.wilmara.com.

TABLE OF CONTENTS

CHAPTER 1

Having a Voice 4

CHAPTER 2

A Somewhat Unpleasant History 8

CHAPTER 3

Women Have Their Say 14

CHAPTER 4

How It's Done 22

THINK ABOUT IT... 30
FOR MORE INFORMATION.................................31
GLOSSARY 32
INDEX... 32

Having a Voice

America is the oldest **democracy** in history. And perhaps the most important privilege in a democracy is the right to vote for the leaders of your government. Voting lets your voice be heard, and it is through the vote that ordinary citizens control the way the country runs. Think about it—if you don't like the way your representatives are doing their job, you can vote them out of office! All elected **politicians**—presidents, senators, governors, mayors, and beyond—have their jobs because voters put them there.

Too many citizens think their one vote won't make much of a difference. But many **elections** have been decided by very small **margins**. Sometimes even a presidential election will come

The right to vote is the main idea of democracy.

George W. Bush won the 2000 election by a very small number of votes.

down to the wire. This happened in 2000. George W. Bush won the presidential election that year over his opponent, Al Gore, by just over 500 votes in Florida! If those votes had gone to Gore, then he would've won the state of Florida, had more electoral votes from all 50 states combined, and become the president instead.

As a right and a privilege, voting should never be taken for granted. There are still countries around the world where people don't have that power. To those people, the United States seems like a dream. Thousands in American history have suffered and died to give us this right, so all people of voting age should exercise that right.

So what's the story behind this wonderful institution called voting? Let's check it out.

21st Century Content

Members of the Senate and the House of Representatives are all elected by the people of their state. They meet with ordinary citizens and listen to their concerns. Then they meet with experts on various subjects, such as agriculture, science, education, and foreign affairs, and try to determine how best to solve their state's problems. In this way, people like you have a voice in the running of their country, demonstrating the true spirit of democracy.

CHAPTER 2

A Somewhat Unpleasant History

Today, any American citizen 18 years or older has the right to cast their vote in an election, as long as they have registered. But this wasn't always the case.

In the earliest days of the United States, only white male adult citizens could vote. They usually had to be property owners, too. This meant that, in many states, if a man rented a house or farm instead of owning it, he was unable to vote. The government finally got rid of the property-ownership requirement in the 1830s. However, the privilege was still only available to white men.

Following the Civil War (1861–1865), the Constitution was changed through the 15th **Amendment** to give African American men voting rights. Unfortunately, not all states

Voting is a much more inclusive process than it used to be.

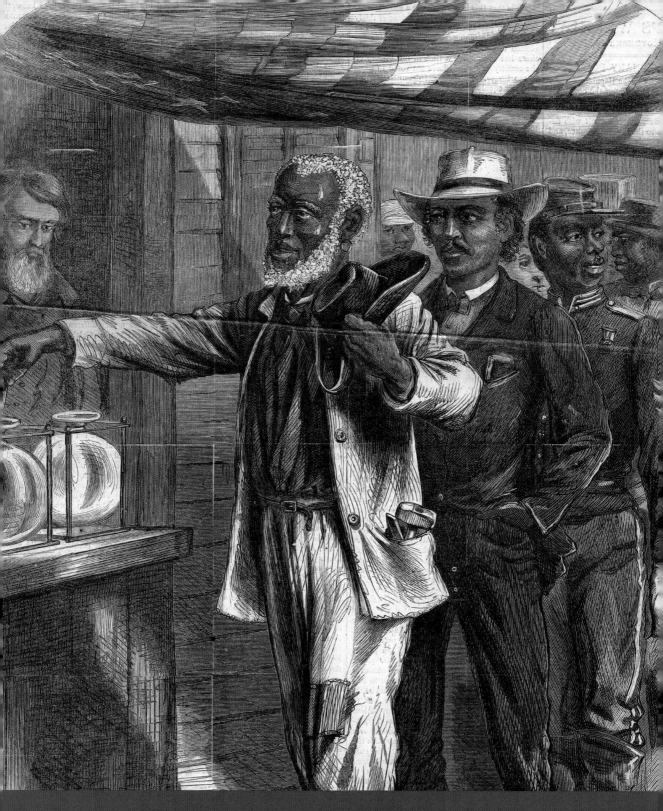

When African Americans were finally allowed to vote, people still put obstacles in their way.

followed the new law. In certain areas of the country, there were people who hated the idea of African American men being able to vote so much that they went out of their way to make sure it didn't happen. Threats and **intimidation** were common methods of stopping it. Another was to require African American males to take a **literacy** test to prove they could read and write. There was even an application to take the test, and it was purposely designed to be complicated and discouraging.

Yet another form of intimidation was the **poll tax**. Its essential function was to make **eligible** voters pay for the right to

Life and Career Skills

A "grandfather" clause to determine eligible voters was enacted by many southern states in 1898, and remained in effect until 1915. It stated that if a man's grandfather was allowed to vote, then so could his descendants. This worked in favor for most white men, but for African Americans, it was used as a way to prevent them from voting. Over time, however, some fair-minded politicians decided to make voting rights equal for everyone. If you were given a political office, what injustices would you work to change? And how would you go about doing it?

During the Vietnam War, the U.S. lowered the voting age from 21 to 18.

vote. Since many African Americans of the time were very poor, they could not afford this tax and thus could not vote. Incredibly, it wasn't until the 1960s that both the literacy test and the poll tax were finally outlawed by the Supreme Court.

In 1971, the voting age in the United States was lowered from 21 to 18 through the 26th Amendment to the Constitution. At that time, thousands of young Americans were fighting in the Vietnam War. Many people argued that if they were old enough to risk their lives for their country, then they were old enough to vote.

Life and Career Skills

A Supreme Court justice has an enormous responsibility to the nation. The cases that the justices vote on are often very complicated. The decisions that each one makes can have a powerful effect on every citizen and become part of history. What qualities do you think a justice needs to have in order to do the job effectively? Which of these qualities do you feel you possess? What is it about you that would make you a good Supreme Court justice?

CHAPTER 3

Women Have Their Say

The great majority of American men had the right to vote by the dawn of the 20th century. Women, on the other hand, were a different story. They couldn't vote no matter how much land they owned or how literate they were. This seemed particularly unfair in a country known as the "land of the free." A fair share of women around this time thought so and decided to do something about it.

American women had been working together in organized groups to fight for their voting rights for quite a while. The first convention to address this issue was held in Seneca Falls, New York, in 1848. The women involved were making good progress until the Civil War flared up and interrupted their efforts. The

FIRST CONVENTION FOR
WOMAN'S RIGHTS
WAS HELD ON THIS CORNER
1848

STATE EDUCATION
DEPARTMENT 1932

In 1848, women advocating for voting rights met in Seneca Falls, New York.

Elizabeth Cady Stanton and Susan B. Anthony worked together as suffragettes.

crusade to give women the right to vote—also known as women's **suffrage**—was set aside so people could concentrate on the war effort. After the war ended, African American men became eligible voters, but women did not.

In 1869, two female-rights activists—Elizabeth Cady Stanton and Susan B. Anthony— founded the National Woman Suffrage Association. They had worked together long before that and formed an influential team, with Stanton

Life and Career Skills

Some nations offer very limited or no voting at all for their citizens. Brunei, for example, is a small island nation in Southeast Asia. The country is an absolute monarchy that is ruled by a sultan. In a monarchy, citizens have no say in governance. The kingdom of Saudi Arabia, in the Middle East, allowed women to vote for the first time in 2015. But not very many did, because of the law against women driving, which made it hard for them to get to the polling places. And the elections were only held for city council members, not for the government's top leaders, who are royalty. How would you feel if you weren't allowed to have any say in who ran your government? What would you try to do to change such a system?

Many men laughed at the idea of women voting.

EXPOSITION:—LET US HAVE A CHAMBER OF FEMALE HORRORS.

The suffragettes marched in parades to draw attention to their cause.

writing powerful speeches and Anthony delivering them to
the public. (Anthony gave about 75 to 100 speeches a year on
the topic of women's rights for more than 40 years!) They were
tireless **advocates** of suffrage, and through their hard work
and dedication, they inspired thousands of others to take up
the same cause.

More women's groups formed. More conventions were held.
Women wrote articles and organized marches. Some women
even tried going to the polls to vote anyway. In fact, in 1872,
Anthony and more than a dozen of her supporters were arrested

In 1920, women were finally allowed to vote.

for attempting to cast their votes. She was convicted of this "crime" and ordered to pay a fine of $100. She refused to do so, and to this day that fine remains unpaid.

By the start of the 20th century, attitudes toward women were beginning to change in America. What helped push this along even further was one of the darkest chapters in American history. After America became involved in World War I, men went overseas to fight. Many women had to take their places in factories and other jobs in order to produce war materials and keep America's economy going. Given the chance to prove their value in the working world, women attained a level of influence and respect they'd never had before. Even U.S. President Woodrow Wilson became a supporter of women's suffrage. Finally, in 1920, all the effort that millions of women had put into the dream of suffrage paid off. The 19th Amendment to the U.S. Constitution, giving women the right to vote, became law.

How It's Done

Elections are held every few years, depending on where you live and which political position is up for a vote. The election for president of the United States, for example, is held every four years (and, interestingly, always in a leap year). Elections for a state's governor are also held every four years, but not necessarily in the same year as the presidential elections. You need to research the details of the election cycles in your town and state before you can vote.

Elections are also held for local political offices. Mayors, judges, city council members, school board members, and others hold positions that voters in towns and cities have a say in. There may even be a position open for the local dogcatcher! Other

City council members are elected to make decisions for the communities where they live.

Bernie Sanders and Hillary Clinton were the two last Democratic presidential candidates in 2016.

elections are held at the state level. The most important and powerful position is the state's governor. There are other elected positions for each state, including senators, representatives, and judges.

Finally, there are national elections, for positions in our federal government. The one you probably know best is for the office of president of the United States. It can be a very exciting event. On those nights, the votes are counted on television as the whole nation watches. And while there is a kind of dramatic, almost theatrical aspect to it, the fact is that it's the end result of a very long and complex process.

In order to cast their vote, voters have to go to their local **polling place**. This will usually be a public building, such as a school, where voting machines are provided. A typical voting machine is a kind of booth with a curtain acting as the door. Voters step into the booth, and the curtain closes around them.

21st Century Content

If you're not living in your home area or you're unable to leave your home to vote, you can still participate in the election process. You can cast what's called an absentee ballot. The rules for this vary from state to state, and the process for getting such a ballot can be a complicated and time consuming. However, all states permit these mail-in ballots under certain circumstances. Many elderly and disabled citizens vote by absentee ballot because they can't physically get to their local polling place. Citizens who are in the military and stationed abroad or who live in foreign countries usually vote by absentee ballot as well.

Voting machines help keep the process organized and accurate.

They slide their **ballot** into the machine. To cast their vote, they might pull small levers by the candidates' names. Or they might have to fill in circles or punch a hole next to their names. Voting machines differ. When done, voters remove the ballot, leave the booth, and place the ballot in a box. More modern voting machines are computerized with touch screens. Some towns prefer to use older machines because computerized systems can be altered, giving false results. And there are still places in

Life and Career Skills

Straight-ticket voting is when a voter stays loyal to one party, usually the Democrats or Republicans. For each election, the voter only chooses candidates from that same party. However, some people are split-ticket voters. This means that they don't feel a strong loyalty to either side, and instead they look at the candidates' views individually. Depending on the issues, they might vote for a Democrat for President but Republicans as other representatives, or another combination. What do you think are the pros and cons of each way of voting? Which one do you think you will do when you're older? Why?

Some polling places still use traditional ballot boxes.

America where people simply write down their choices on ballots and drop them in a box.

In small towns across the nation, voters attend town meetings and then cast their votes either by ballot or voice. Town meetings are held at least once a year, and all qualified voters are encouraged to attend. The meetings are usually held in school auditoriums or some other venue large enough to comfortably host everyone. Typical issues discussed include the town's budget and other monetary topics, repairs and upgrades, appointments, and raises for public employees.

Think About It

Some countries, such as Australia, have a law that all of their citizens over a certain age have to vote. Anyone who doesn't must pay a fine. Do you agree with this law? Why or why not?

Ask your parents or older siblings who they voted for in the most recent election. Why did they choose this candidate instead of the others? What issues are the most important to them? How did they feel when this candidate won or lost the election? (But be polite! They might not want to talk about it, and that's okay. Some people like to keep who they vote for a secret.)

For More Information

BOOKS

Cunningham, Kevin. *How Political Campaigns and Elections Work.* Edina, MN: ABDO, 2015.

Goodman, Susan E., and Elwood Smith (illustrator). *See How They Run: Campaign Dreams, Election Schemes, and the Race to the White House.* New York: Bloomsbury, 2012.

Winter, Jonah, and Barry Blitt (illustrator). *The Founding Fathers! The Horse-Ridin', Fiddle-Playin', Book-Readin', Gun-Totin' Gentlemen Who Started America.* New York: Atheneum, 2015.

ON THE WEB

Congress for Kids—Elections: Political Parties
www.congressforkids.net/Elections_politicalparties.htm

Kids.gov—Government
https://kids.usa.gov/government/index.shtml

PBS Parents—Helping Kids Understand the Elections
www.pbs.org/parents/special/election/article-theraceison.html

GLOSSARY

advocates (AD-vuh-kits) people who support an idea or plan

amendment (uh-MEND-muhnt) a change made to a bill

ballot (BAL-uht) a way of voting secretly, using a machine or a slip of paper

democracy (dih-MAH-kruh-see) a form of government in which the people choose their leaders in elections

elections (ih-LEK-shuhnz) the act of choosing someone or deciding something by voting

eligible (EL-ih-juh-buhl) having the right abilities or qualifications for something

intimidation (in-tim-ih-DAY-shuhn) the act of frightening someone in order to make that person do something

literacy (LIT-ur-uh-see) the ability to read and write

margins (MAHR-jinz) an amount by which something wins or falls short

politicians (pah-lih-TISH-uhns) people who run for or hold a government office

polling place (POHL-ing plase) the place where votes are cast and recorded during an election

poll tax (POHL TAKS) a fixed amount of money a person is charged for the right to vote

suffrage (SUHF-rij) the right to vote

INDEX

absentee ballots, 25
African Americans, 8, 10–11, 17
Anthony, Susan B., 16, 17, 19, 21

ballots, 25, 27, 28, 29

democracy, 4, 5, 7

elections, 4, 6, 8, 17, 22–29

literacy tests, 11, 13

poll tax, 11, 13
polling places, 25, 28

Seneca Falls, NY, 14, 15
Stanton, Elizabeth Cady, 16, 17, 19
suffragettes, 16, 17, 19

Vietnam War, 12, 13

voting, 4–7
  age, 12, 13
  history, 8–13
  how it's done, 22–29
  rights, 5, 6–7, 14
  straight-ticket, 27

white men, 8, 11
women, 14–21
World War I, 21